Humanitarian Needs
Assessment

T0266356

Praise for this book

'When crisis, strife and misery are at their worst we need to know what is needed to start saving lives and help people help themselves. Based on the advice of so many who have lived through these worst of circumstances we now have this guideline for those who need it the most: field-based staff and national responders. They are the first to respond in their own communities and this guideline will enable them to provide the critical information needed to inform the wider humanitarian community.'

Jan Egeland
Secretary General, Norwegian Refugee Council

'*Humanitarian Needs Assessment – The Good Enough Guide* is a very welcome addition to the needs assessment support literature that is available, and gives humanitarian practitioners a step-by-step tool with clear and practical recommendations to help them carry out assessments in the field.'

Claus Sørensen,
Director-General, DG Humanitarian Aid and Civil Protection, European Commission

Humanitarian Needs Assessment

The Good Enough Guide

The Assessment Capacities Project
and Emergency Capacity Building
Project

PRACTICAL ACTION
Publishing

Practical Action Publishing Ltd
The Schumacher Centre, Bourton on Dunsmore, Rugby,
Warwickshire CV23 9QZ, UK
www.practicalactionpublishing.org

© Norwegian Refugee Council, 2014

ISBN 978-1-85339-862-9 Hardback

ISBN 978-1-85339-863-6 Paperback

ISBN 978-1-78044-862-6 Library Ebook

ISBN 978-1-78044-863-3 Ebook

Citation: ACAPS (2014) *Humanitarian Needs Assessment: The Good
Enough Guide*, The Assessment Capacities Project (ACAPS), Emergency
Capacity Building Project (ECB) and Practical Action Publishing, Rugby, UK.
<http://dx.doi.org/10.3362/9781780448626>

Since 1974, Practical Action Publishing has published and
disseminated books and information in support of international
development work throughout the world. Practical Action Publishing
is a trading name of Practical Action Publishing Ltd (Company Reg.
No. 1159018), the wholly owned publishing company of Practical
Action. Practical Action Publishing trades only in support of its
parent charity objectives and any profits are covenanted back to
Practical Action (Charity Reg. No. 247257,
Group VAT Registration No. 880 9924 76).

Cover design by Mercer Design
Typeset by Allzone Digital Services Limited
Printed by Hussar Books

FSC
www.fsc.org
MIX
Paper from
responsible sources
FSC® C115691

Contents

http://dx.doi.org/10.3362/9781780448626.000

Acknowledgements

Humanitarian Needs Assessment – The Good Enough Guide was developed through wide-ranging consultations which began in November 2012. Input was through workshops and field tests and by face-to-face, email and phone discussions. The Assessment Capacities Project (ACAPS) and The Emergency Capacity Building Project (ECB) would like to thank the following people for having contributed to this book:

Paul Currion, the author.

Patrice Chataigner, Sandie Walton-Ellery and Susan Erb, for technical input and revisions.

Jock Backer, Megan Chisholm, Hana Crowe, Richard Garfield, Shagufta Jeelani, Lars Peter Nissen and Angela Rouse for their valuable input as members of the steering committee.

Laure Anquez, Massimo Altimari, Graziella Ito-Pellegri, Jennifer Price-Jones and Sandie Walton-Ellery, for facilitating feedback workshops in Bolivia, Kenya and Bangladesh.

David Hockaday, Jonathan Hanson, Judith Burchett, Jane Linekar, Caroline Draveny and Rolf M. Bakken for supporting the process of seeing the guide into publication.

ACAPS and ECB also gratefully acknowledge those who contributed their expertise and provided feedback during the drafting and piloting phase. We received comments and feedback from over 150 individuals and organizations, all of which strengthened the content of the guide significantly.

Preface: Why and how to use *Humanitarian Needs Assessment – The Good Enough Guide*

Why

Needs assessment is essential for programme planning, monitoring and evaluation, and **accountability**, however needs assessment is still a critical weakness of humanitarian response. Organizations urgently need to improve how they do assessments.

The humanitarian community has been working on this issue through a number of different initiatives. The focus has been on coordinated needs assessments (CNA), sometimes referred to as joint needs assessment (JNA).

The inter-agency Needs Assessment Task Force has issued an operational guidance note which provides useful technical advice. It has also developed the Multi Cluster/Sector Initial Rapid Assessment (MIRA), which is now being used in a number of locations. Details of where to access these documents are in the resources section of this guide.

However, individual staff members with responsibility for carrying out needs assessments have had few practical resources to help them. The Assessment Capacities Project (ACAPS) and the Emergency Capacity Building Project (ECB) have produced this guide to fill the gap that existed for a practical resource that pulls together the main lessons learned from various initiatives and experiences.

Who

This guide is written for field staff carrying out assessments in the early days and weeks following a disaster. It is especially aimed at national project managers and their teams.

When

The steps and tools in this guide are most directly useful for initial and rapid assessments in the first weeks of an emergency, but the principles and practices described apply at any stage in the response. Be flexible depending on your situation and the needs and capacities of disaster-affected communities.

How

This guide does not explain every activity that you will need to carry out for your assessment, but it will help you through the assessment process. You can use it to take you through the whole assessment or to help at particular points in the process.

The guide has three sections to help you with assessments: *steps*, *tools*, and *resources*.

- Each *step* describes a part of the assessment cycle (see Figure 1) and guides you through it.
- Each *tool* helps you with specific activities that are part of carrying out a step.
- Each *resource* directs you to information that will help you learn more about assessment.

Under *resources*, a glossary is included defining terminology particular to assessments and used throughout
the book. When a term is used that is further explained
in the glossary, it is marked in bold, and (for electronic
versions) hyperlinked. References to *tools* are also
marked in bold and hyperlinked.

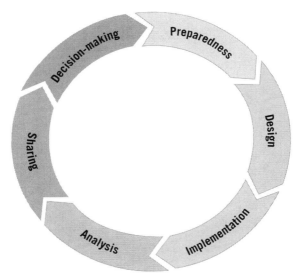

Figure 1. The assessment cycle

CHAPTER ONE

WHAT IS NEEDS ASSSESSMENT?

This chapter looks at what a needs assessment is, and provides you with some basic principles of assessments.

Keywords: needs assessment, decision-making, disaster, coordination, principles

What is...?

Needs assessment

Needs assessment is how organizations identify and measure the humanitarian needs of a disaster-affected community. Simply put, needs assessment is the best way to answer the question: 'What assistance do disaster-affected communities need?'

Needs assessments use various methods to collect and analyse information. These enable the organization to make good decisions about how to allocate resources and gather more resources to meet the needs of the disaster-affected community.

Decision-making

Organizations need to make decisions as they work out how to allocate their resources to meet their goals. The

http://dx.doi.org/10.3362/9781780448626.001

main goal of humanitarian organizations is to support disaster-affected communities. Decision-making happens at every level in an organization, for various reasons.

Box 1. Why might an organization carry out a needs assessment?

- To work out what the organization's most important goals are.
- To plan technical programmes.
- To prepare proposals for fundraising.
- To develop the right advocacy messages.
- To design later assessments with more detail.

In emergencies, needs assessments make good decision-making possible. They do this by putting information together to build up a full picture of the needs of the disaster-affected community. Needs assessments provide the evidence that helps senior decision-makers in the field (such as project managers and country directors) to make good decisions.

A disaster-affected community

In this guide, 'disaster-affected communities' and/ or 'disaster-affected individuals' refer to all members of a community that has been affected by a natural disaster or complex emergency. It includes everyone in the community regardless of age, disability, ethnicity, gender, HIV and AIDS status, religion, sexual orientation, social standing, or how much the disaster affects them.

Good enough

In this guide, being 'good enough' means choosing a simple solution rather than a complicated one. 'Good enough' does *not* mean second best. In an emergency response, a quick and simple approach to needs assessment may be the only practical possibility. When the situation changes, review your approach and change it to deal with the current situation.

Basic principles of needs assessment

Make the scope of the assessment reflect the size and nature of the crisis

- Do not overextend the assessment, especially in the early phases. Make it wide enough to indicate the full situation but narrow enough to be manageable.
- Consider all technical sectors: water, sanitation, hygiene (WASH), food security, health, shelter, protection, and so on.
- Consider the operating environment: environmental, social, economic, and security factors.
- Set baselines for measuring the impact of the disaster.
- When you set these baselines, note any chronic needs that existed *before* the disaster.

Produce timely and relevant analysis

- Do the first assessment as soon as possible after the disaster.
- Before you do the assessment, identify the specific decisions it must help with.

- Review existing data before you decide whether to collect new data.

- Check data against other sources.

- Present the minimum data needed to make the specific decisions you have identified.

- Distribute the findings and analysis quickly to support decision-making and further assessments.

Collect usable data

- **Disaggregate** your data to a level that will enable decision-makers to understand the different effects of the disaster on different groups.

- Disaggregate on a geographical basis, cross-check population figures against as many sources as possible, and disaggregate those figures by sex and age.

Box 2. What do I need to know about coordinated assessments?

Organizations now often strive to conduct a coordinated needs assessment (CNA) in the first phases of an emergency response. CNAs are usually coordinated by a central body, often a government agency, the UN Office for Coordination of Humanitarian Affairs (OCHA), an inter-agency body like an assessment working group, a **cluster**, or a group of non-governmental organizations (NGOs). They identify top shared priorities for the whole humanitarian community.

(continued)

Box 2. What do I need to know about coordinated assessments? (continued)

You are unlikely to be responsible for coordinating a large-scale CNA, but your organization may take part in one. The basic principles of a CNA are the same as for any assessment. The difference is that it will involve multiple organizations working alongside each other. There are two ways they can do this:

- In a *joint assessment*, different organizations use a single tool and methodology to carry out the assessment with a single set of results. Joint assessments are more useful in the first weeks of a sudden-onset disaster to gain a rapid overview of a situation.

- In a *harmonized assessment*, different organizations use their own tools and methodologies but share and compare assessment results so that they can do joint analysis. Harmonized assessments are more useful in the months following a disaster or in longer-term, complex emergencies.

Being an effective partner in a CNA means two things:

- You are not passive. You are actively involved in developing the assessment process and encouraging other organizations to do the same. This will help to ensure that the CNA is useful for your organization and for others that share your goals.

- You make sure your organization uses the outputs of the CNA, incorporates the findings into its own programming, and participates in any joint planning that follows from the CNA.

Use valid and transparent methods

- Use standardized data collection techniques and procedures for analysing data.

- Standardized procedures should lead to accurate data and sound conclusions, but always check your findings against other assessments and similar data from a variety of sources.

- Make your methodology public, including any assumptions you rely on in your analysis, limitations on the accuracy of your data, and the sources you have used. This lets others judge the quality of the data.

Be accountable

- Make sure disaster-affected communities are involved in planning, implementing, and judging the response.

- To do this you must set up processes that give communities and individuals a voice in the assessment.

Coordinate with others and share findings

- Talk with other organizations doing assessments.

- Make sure other stakeholders know that you are doing an assessment.

- Participate in coordinated needs assessments where possible – i.e. if there is a coordinated assessment that your organization is able to be part of, and if the focus of that assessment suits your organization's aims and activities.

Box 3. When is it a good idea to take a coordinated approach to needs assessment?

Even if there is no CNA organized, it is always good to consider coordinating your assessment with partners if possible. Working together helps to create a shared understanding of the situation, to facilitate a coordinated and more effective response, and to use assessment resources more efficiently (for example, by sharing logistics arrangements).

The advantages of a CNA are:

- Fewer gaps and duplications in assessment coverage.

- More efficient use of resources, enabling organizations to cover more locations.

- Less chance of assessment fatigue in disaster-affected communities.

Other points to consider are:

- Only coordinate with organizations that share your organization's values and principles.

- Only coordinate with organizations that you already have or want to build a working relationship with.

- Avoid a coordinated approach if it might compromise your organization's humanitarian principles.

(continued)

- If the mandate for your assessment is specific to your organization, you may not be able to do a coordinated assessment. However, you may still decide to share assessment findings so that you can provide better assistance.

- Make sure the working relationship is clear, particularly about which partner has responsibility for which activities. Be clear about the specific value that you and your partners add to the overall assessment. You may need a formal agreement (for example, a memorandum of understanding) between the organizations involved.

- Make findings available to other sectors, national authorities, and representatives of disaster-affected communities.

- Structure and write your reports in a way that helps the readers to prioritize issues and take action.

Make sure you can get enough resources

You may need to form and train an assessment team and support them with logistics, transport, communications, accommodation, and so on. You need your organization to fully support the assessment (**Tool 1**).

Assess local capacities

- Consider how the local and national authorities and other groups are responding.

- Identify capacities and strategies the disaster-affected community and surrounding population are using to cope with the disaster.
- In particular, you must consider gender, age and specific vulnerabilities (such as disability). Your methods, analysis and selection of team members must take into account the different needs, vulnerabilities, capacities and perspectives of women and men, boys and girls.

Manage community expectations

- Avoid building unrealistic expectations in disaster-affected communities of what your assessment will lead to.
- Manage the expectations of other stakeholders, including local authorities and assessment partners.
- Avoid creating assessment fatigue in disaster-affected communities. Multiple visits without visible outcomes create assessment fatigue and unrealistic expectations.
- Be sensitive to cultural norms, individual privacy and the potential psychological impact of your assessment.

Remember that assessment is not just a one-off event

- Continue assessment throughout the emergency.
- Collect data in increasing detail.
- Refine the assessment and update your findings as the situation changes.

CHAPTER TWO

STEPS TO A GOOD ENOUGH NEEDS ASSESSMENT

This chapter takes you through all the steps of an assessment cycle from preparedness and planning, to reporting and dissemination of findings. Each section focuses on how to efficiently carry out one step, and provides tips and links to useful tools.

Keywords: preparedness, design, implementation, analysis, reporting

http://dx.doi.org/10.3362/9781780448626.002

Step 1: Preparing for an assessment

Before the emergency

Make sure your organization has assessment procedures that fit with its contingency plans and programme planning (**Tool 2**). The plan should explain how your organization will carry out the assessment from start to finish, what the different parts of the organization are responsible for, and how it will balance cost, speed and quality.

Identify, check and be ready to mobilize the staff and other resources that you will need to implement the assessment (**Tool 1**). A review of **secondary data** may only need one or two people (and can often be done by staff outside the affected area). **Primary data** collection will need more staff, support and funding.

Make sure you know how to get an assessment started in your organization: is there a formal process, or does it only need informal approval from a senior manager? How you mobilize resources will depend on your organization and your position in it, but you will need senior management support to secure those resources and to establish procedures in advance (for example, recruiting or seconding staff to assessment teams). You may need to persuade senior managers that it is important to be prepared for an assessment. You can do this by emphasizing that it is more cost-effective to prepare in advance.

During and after the emergency

Your organization should plan its response based on evidence that gives you a clear understanding of the situation. Needs assessment is the main way to gather that evidence. You can define your assessment using four questions:

1. Should your organization intervene, and what value will it add to the response?
2. What should the nature, scale and details of your intervention be?
3. How should you prioritize and allocate resources strategically?
4. What practical actions should the programme design and planning involve?

Before you decide what sort of assessment to do, think carefully about the following:

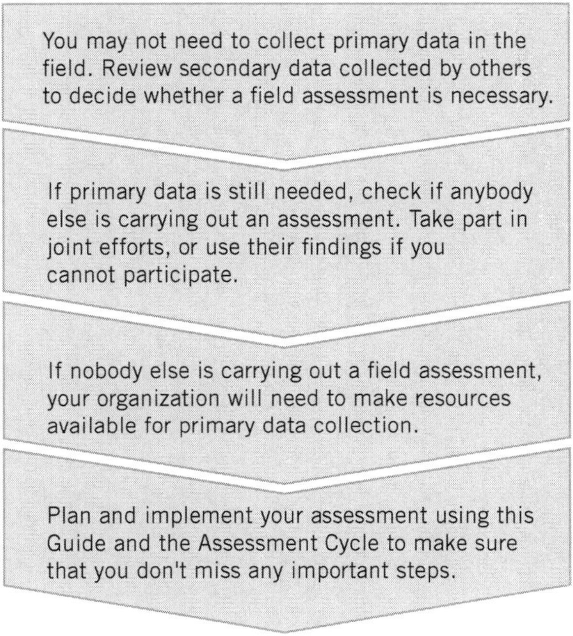

You may not need to collect primary data in the field. Review secondary data collected by others to decide whether a field assessment is necessary.

If primary data is still needed, check if anybody else is carrying out an assessment. Take part in joint efforts, or use their findings if you cannot participate.

If nobody else is carrying out a field assessment, your organization will need to make resources available for primary data collection.

Plan and implement your assessment using this Guide and the Assessment Cycle to make sure that you don't miss any important steps.

Figure 2. Assessment considerations

Step 2: Designing your assessment

There is no single methodology for an assessment that meets every information need in every situation.

You can apply the good practice described in this guide to develop simple, flexible and robust approaches adapted to your specific needs and the capacities of your organization. You should review existing tools, mechanisms and lessons learned from your own and other organizations to avoid reinventing the wheel or repeating past mistakes.

Get the basic facts

An assessment must include information about three key elements:

1. *Where*: locations where the impact has been greatest and/or is likely to be greatest.
2. *Who*: groups most in need of humanitarian assistance and/or most vulnerable.
3. *What*: sectors that require immediate action and/or ongoing attention.

Engage stakeholders

You will need to engage stakeholders, especially decision-makers who will use the assessment findings and (if possible) the communities who will be involved in the assessment. Stakeholders should be clear about what the assessment is meant to achieve and produce, their role in the assessment process, and how they can use the assessment findings to help with their decisions.

Support specific decisions

Every assessment should be designed to enable the organization to make specific decisions. The following five questions will help you to provide the right information to the right people at the right time:

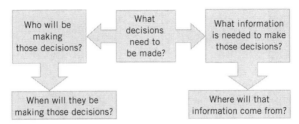

Figure 3. Supporting decision-makers

Be realistic

Design your assessment to fit the amount and types of resources you can mobilize. The assessment should be big enough to meet identified decision-making requirements, but the costs of collecting data should not outweigh the benefits of having it.

The more ambitious, the more costly, and less timely the assessment, the greater the chance of failure.

Review secondary data

A secondary data review should identify what information already exists. This may be information previously collected by your own organization or by other organizations (**Tool 6**).

Collect primary data if necessary

Once secondary data has been reviewed, if there are significant information gaps, you will need to collect primary data in the field (**Tool 7**).

Keep the process going

Needs assessment is not just a one-off event; it evolves as the situation changes in the weeks and months following a disaster. The focus of a needs assessment will change as the response unfolds and decision-makers require information on new issues.

Each assessment should build on previous assessments, since the information required becomes more detailed, sector specific and long term as the response develops.

Step 3: Implementing your assessment

An assessment will only be successful with effective leadership and careful management. Keep your objectives and deliverables clear, and measure your progress against them continuously.

The situation may change quickly in an emergency, so remain flexible and be ready to update the assessment to suit new circumstances. Changes may be *inside* your organization as new priorities are decided – for example, partnership with a government ministry. Or they may be *outside* your organization as new events occur – for example, a resurgence in an ongoing conflict.

You will face many challenges (see Table 1), but your assessment does not have to be perfect to be useful. An imperfect assessment is better than no assessment, as long as its imperfections are made clear.

Use a standardized, transparent and clearly documented process; follow recognized data collection methods; use widely accepted terms from the humanitarian sector; and apply relevant technical standards and indicators. This will enable others to assess the credibility and reliability of your findings, and make it possible to compare those findings with other assessments.

Table 1. Potential challenges and solutions

Challenge	Example of the challenge	Example of a solution
Preparedness	Lack of (or poorly organized) pre-crisis data may make it difficult to gather secondary data.	Arrange a meeting of key stakeholders to share information from their organizations.
Logistics	Distance, insecurity or lack of infrastructure may make it difficult to access affected areas.	Develop a logistics plan (including security issues) that minimizes risks to the assessment.
Communications	Language barriers or telecommunications problems may make it difficult to communicate with disaster-affected communities.	Ensure that your assessment team has the necessary language skills and adequate communications equipment.

(continued)

Table 1. Potential challenges and solutions *(continued)*

Challenge	Example of the challenge	Example of a solution
Comparison	Different approaches used by different organizations may make it difficult to compare data.	Participate in any coordination mechanisms (for example, clusters) or joint assessments. Talk with colleagues in other organizations regularly. Ensure that colleagues are using the same definitions and standards (for example, **P-codes**).
Capacity	Lack of skilled or trained assessment staff may make it difficult to carry out the assessment.	Train staff members in assessment skills before an emergency strikes and use simple, easy-to-understand questionnaires.
Acceptance	Local authorities or the community itself may be unwilling to participate in the assessment.	Arrange a multi-stakeholder meeting to communicate the importance of the assessment.

Consultation and accountability

Coordinate with stakeholders (particularly national and local governments) and work with partners (such as local NGOs and community groups) to design and implement the assessment. Carrying out a stakeholder analysis may be helpful where you identify and make an overview of all the stakeholders or interest groups associated with this assessment and how they may be influenced by the outcome. This will help you determine who you should work closely with, and who you only need to keep informed.

Engage these stakeholders as early as possible, and communicate with them frequently throughout the process – for example, call them regularly to ask for technical input and guidance, email sample questionnaires, or hold consultation meetings. This engagement will help them to feel ownership of any assessment findings. However, be careful not to overload them with requests or information.

Disaster-affected communities are also stakeholders in the assessment (**Tool 5**). Political and community leaders will not be able to give the complete picture of how a disaster has affected the community. The assessment should try to represent *all* groups of the affected population, especially those who may be vulnerable.

Who is vulnerable?

Vulnerability is the result of many factors (**Tool 8**). **Tool 9** explains how to organize a field visit, but it may be difficult to reach and consult all vulnerable individuals and communities during an initial assessment because of the factors illustrated below.

WHERE THEY ARE	WHO THEY ARE	WHAT THEY HAVE EXPERIENCED
They may live in places that are less accessible, such as slums or unofficial camps, or be difficult to reach by vehicle.	They may belong to marginalised groups, such as people with disabilities or older people.	They may have experiences that are difficult to talk about, such as gender-based violence.

Figure 4. Why is it difficult to reach some individuals or communities?

You should keep notes on which groups have been left out, list them in your report, and make plans to cover them at the earliest opportunity (**Tool 8**). You should also consult host communities, who may feel the impact of the arrival of communities displaced by the disaster.

The assessment team

Your assessment team is your most important resource, because the trustworthiness of the results depends on the quality of the team. The more qualified and experienced an assessment team is, the more accurate and reliable the assessment findings will be.

Choose team members who have the skills and experience you require to respond to this particular disaster (**Tool 3**), and make the skills and competences complement each other.

If possible, team members should be staff recruited specifically for the assessment, or existing staff who are seconded to the team. Before the emergency, recruit and train the team in the assessment skills and tools they will be using. If they have the opportunity to work together, it will make them more effective and save time during the assessment (**Tool 4**).

You must understand your team's strengths and weaknesses (based on characters, skills and experience) when assigning roles and tasks.

In particular your team must be willing and able to engage communities in a culturally acceptable manner. Staff may be from an ethnic or religious group that is not well perceived, or they may have prejudices about other ethnic or religious groups. You can address these problems by:

- ensuring that your team has a range of backgrounds, including ethnic and religious;
- ensuring that your team has an appropriate balance of male and female members;
- making team members aware of their prejudices, and enabling team leaders to challenge such views; and
- training team members in specific methods to engage with communities in an appropriate way.

Based on the assessment plan, you should agree on standard operating procedures (SOPs) with key stakeholders. SOPs describe the roles and responsibilities of team members, the team's management lines and support functions, and clearly identify team leaders (**Tool 10**). The team must understand the SOPs and be able to communicate key points to affected communities.

Collecting data

Secondary data is existing data that your organization or others have already collected (**Tool 6**). A secondary data review is the first step to:

- build awareness of the current situation;
- establish a baseline for measuring the impact of the disaster;
- create the opportunity to explore potential outcomes through scenario building;
- identify information gaps that future assessments can fill; and
- select sites and target populations for assessment.

An assessment should start by collecting secondary data. It should then go on to collect primary data *only* if necessary. Collecting secondary data takes less time, money and effort than collecting primary data. Much of the data you need may already be available from secondary data sources, although you must decide whether it is of good enough quality to base your analysis on.

Primary data is new data that your organization collects directly from the field, through direct observation, key informant interviews, community group discussions and other tools (**Tool 7**). It may be needed to fill information gaps identified during your secondary data review. The amount and quality of primary data available will increase over time as more locations are assessed. Primary data will not usually be the main source of information until after the first weeks of a crisis. Until then you should use it to confirm secondary data, not the other way around.

The 'good enough' principle applies to the data you collect as well as the way you collect it. Do not collect more data than necessary to make the key decisions that you have already identified. Particularly in the early days and weeks of a disaster, avoid adding too many questions to an assessment to satisfy a specific department or sector. Ask them to say what they need that data for, and check if it is possible to gather it from another source or at a later stage. You can defend your decision by explaining that this assessment will not be the only opportunity to gather data, and that resources are limited and need to be targeted very efficiently.

Box 4. Some things to avoid

Don't ask individuals to comment on issues specific to their household (for example, the volume of water they have access to) since this is of limited use in early phases of a crisis. Focus on community-level issues to ensure the assessment reflects collective needs.

Don't cover an area larger than a community (district or sub-district level) in your primary data collection. It may be too broad to be useful in determining priority needs of affected populations. Keep your geographical scope limited to a specific community or area.

Don't ask technical questions about a particular sector, as they can be misunderstood by non-specialists. Establish the critical information needed to understand the general needs of the population and make decisions to meet those needs.

Step 4: Analysing your data

Analysis involves the combination of available information and its interpretation. Analysis begins by comparing data from different locations and/or groups as shown in the Table 2, below, to identify similarities and differences. These can help you understand how the situation has developed and will develop. This makes it possible to prioritize groups, locations and sectors, leading to recommendations for the response.

Analysis should start as soon as you begin to receive data (secondary or primary) and continue as long as you are receiving new data. Test and revise your analysis against new data as it comes in and new sources as they are identified. Keep track of data and sources so that you can refer back to them.

Table 2. Examples of comparisons

What am I comparing?	Between	And
Locations	Rural	Urban
Locations	Province A	Province B
Livelihoods	Wage workers	Farmers
Population groups	Residents	Internally displaced people
Settings	Camps	Host communities
Affected population	Male	Female
Affected population	Children / older people	General population
Time	Pre-disaster	Post-disaster

Analysis benefits from a range of perspectives from different genders, ages, ethnicities, etc., so every staff member can contribute to analysis, starting with the assessment team.

What is useful analysis for one organization or sector might not be useful for another, since they will have different decision-making needs. However, your analysis should contribute to a shared picture of the situation that can be used by all humanitarian actors – not just your organization. When you present your analysis, emphasize that it is a dynamic but incomplete picture that will be revised if and when you receive new data.

The complex and unpredictable nature of humanitarian emergencies, combined with the limited availability of data, makes precision and accuracy more difficult. Make clear what data your analysis is based on, and the source of that data. Be honest about gaps in your data, and explain the reasons for those gaps – lack of access, resources, etc. This will help you and others to plan future assessments, build scenarios, and allocate resources efficiently.

When possible, your analysis should also identify gaps in **capacity**: human resources, aid materials, logistics capabilities, coping strategies, etc. What resources exist to meet the needs you identify? What additional resources are needed? This includes resources available to the affected communities, the local and national authorities, and international actors.

Checking your findings

Validation is the continuous process of comparing information that you have collected with information from other sources. It is not about *proving* your findings; it is about providing an interpretation that fits your findings. The validity of your findings will be judged on:

- how strong your arguments are;
- the quality of the evidence you provide;
- how much cross-checking of findings you have done;
- the quality of the methodology; and
- the reputation of those involved.

At its simplest, validation means checking information from a key informant against information from other key informants, or validating data collected by one assessment team member against data collected by other team members. Table 3 describes four ways to validate your findings.

Table 3. Validating your findings

1. Cross-checking (or 'triangulation'). Different organizations may use different methods to arrive at a particular figure, for example, population estimates. Comparing these against each other will help you make your own estimate.	2. Convergence. If different pieces of evidence from independent sources are pointing to one conclusion, that conclusion is more likely to be accurate. If some evidence contradicts other evidence, you will need to reconcile them to understand what is happening.
3. Consultation. If you involve stakeholders with varied expertise in analysing the data, you will gain a wider perspective and a stronger consensus. However, you will need to balance this against any biases that these stakeholders might have.	4. Confidence. If you balance the strength of your evidence with the level of agreement among stakeholders, you gain a higher level of confidence in your findings.

Step 5: Sharing your findings

Once you have collected and analysed the data, share the findings to increase a shared understanding of the situation and help with decisions (**Tool 14**). Make your findings available to:

- colleagues (within your organization);
- peers (in other organizations);
- coordinators (government, cluster or other);
- local and national authorities; and
- affected communities.

Writing your report

You will usually be expected to present your findings in an assessment report. **Tool 15** gives you a suggested structure for the report. The report must, however, include three major components:

1. findings (including background context);
2. analysis of those findings to explain what is happening; and
3. methodology for how you collected your data and carried out your analysis.

Make your reports as user-friendly as possible. Shorter documents are more likely to be read. Write as little as possible, but as much as you need to communicate your findings. Clearly define key terms to avoid mis-understanding – for example, what does *disaster-affected* mean? Start with an executive summary, highlight key points, use bullet points, identify your sources in footnotes, and include visual aids, for example, maps and graphs.

Every assessment has assumptions, limitations, biases and gaps. Acknowledging these helps others understand how you reached your conclusions. You should share your methodology in your report, and state your level of confidence in your findings. This is important for transparency and accountability, since it enables others to judge your assessment for themselves, and ensures that other stakeholders (particularly those arriving in later phases) understand clearly what you have done.

A written assessment report is not the only way to communicate your findings. You may need to create other products, such as briefing notes and slide presentations. Different users require different levels of detail in different formats.

Presenting your findings

You should present your analysis in a form that meets the expectations and requirements of the target audience. Before you start writing, ask what information they need, how they want it to be presented, and how often they would like it updated. Think about who will use your findings (for example, colleagues in your organization, peers in other organizations, other assessment teams, and the next person in your job) and shape your reporting to their needs.

You can also use the sharing process to start discussions with key stakeholders. This can be a good way to get feedback on your reports, support for your recommendations, and develop a shared understanding of the situation.

In a rapidly changing situation, the data you collect may quickly be out of date. How quickly you share your findings may therefore be more important than how much detail is in them. Do not wait until all information is available from all areas, or until information has been verified and analysed, or until you produce a final report. Instead, share your findings and methodology with other organizations as early as possible. Make it clear that the findings are provisional, and provide updates on your progress all through the assessment.

You should share your findings widely and quickly, but be aware of security and safety concerns. Your assessment may affect disaster-affected communities, particularly in conflict situations or where there are unresolved political issues. You may need to prepare two versions of a report: one for internal use and another for public distribution. You may need to restrict access to your data if releasing it widely would create specific and obvious risks to disaster-affected communities. These are complicated issues, so consult the communities, staff in your organization, and any relevant coordinating body before you openly share data.

Helping with decision-making

Assessment findings should be useful for making decisions. Think about how you can make your findings most useful to decision-makers, and what will make the most difference to disaster-affected communities. Your assessment is more likely to be used if you present the findings in a way that explains very clearly the impact of the crisis and how the crisis might develop. Answer the questions that decision-makers will have, such as:

- How are pre-crisis vulnerabilities likely to be affected by the disaster?
- What is known about the impact of similar disasters or crises in the region in the past?
- What does this tell us about the potential evolution of the disaster?
- What coping strategies are in place and how can these be supported?
- What factors or **drivers** could contribute to worsening conditions?
- Is there a need for external assistance, and what are the appropriate responses?
- What are the potential transition and/or exit strategies?

Be prepared to defend any conclusions you draw and recommendations you make. You can indicate what you think is the most suitable response but you should primarily present the evidence to allow decision-makers to draw their own conclusions. It can be useful to think about how your findings can be used to support the full range of organizational requirements: logistics, human resources, monitoring and evaluation, fundraising, etc.

CHAPTER THREE

TOOLS

This chapter contains checklists, tables and other tools to help you at specific stages of the assessment process.

Keywords: planning, training, data collection, sampling, technology

http://dx.doi.org/10.3362/9781780448626.003

Tool 1: How do I prepare my organization for an assessment?

Having systems in place before an emergency happens allows you to respond more quickly and effectively. Start by reviewing existing tools, mechanisms, capacities, and lessons learned from previous crises and assessments. Integrate assessment preparations into the following organizational areas.

Table 4. Which organizational areas support assessment?

Organizational area	Critical questions
Management commitment	Does your senior management understand the importance of needs assessment in the humanitarian response?
Organizational support	• Do you have support from at least one key figure in your senior management? • Is there someone who can help you to get the resources necessary for assessment?
Contingency planning	• Is assessment included in your organizational contingency plans? • If you carry out contingency or simulation exercises, do they include assessment? • Is there a process for using assessment findings to verify and update contingency plans?

(continued)

Table 4. Which organizational areas support assessment
(continued)

Staff develop-ment	• Do your staff have the opportu-nity to be trained in assessment skills? • Can less experienced staff be mentored by or partnered with more experienced staff? • Are assessment skills included in internal staff training packages?
Human resources (HR)	• Do job descriptions for key field staff include experience in carrying out assessments? • Are your HR systems flexible enough to recruit and deploy assessment teams rapidly?
Logistics planning	• Are enough resources (for example, transport and commu-nications) available to support assessment teams? • Will you have enough access to and authority over those resources throughout the assessment?
Security plans	• Are your security staff involved in the assessment process, and will they be available during the assessment?

(continued)

Table 4. Which organizational areas support assessment
(continued)

Security plans	• Are there security measures to ensure the safety of assessment teams?
Organi-zational learning	• Is your assessment clearly linked to any future monitoring and evaluation strategy? • Are you documenting the assessment to make sure that lessons can be learned?
Can you think of any others?	

Tool 2: How do I develop an assessment plan?

Your assessment plan should contain five elements:

1. **Objectives:** Terms of Reference with measurable goals and clear objectives, timeframe (including delivery dates and reporting frequency), the specific deliverables and which decisions they will inform.

2. **Scope:** What data do you need to gather? Work with stakeholders to state their specific information needs. Table 5 shows the most common requirements.

Table 5. Identifying and addressing problems

What are the *problems*?	<ul><li>Which people have been affected by the emergency? *(Group)*</li><li>What are their greatest needs in terms of life-saving assistance? *(Sector)*</li><li>Where are the most affected areas? *(Location)*</li></ul>
What are the *sources* of the problems?	<ul><li>What has the impact of the disaster been?</li><li>What vulnerabilities exist?</li><li>What capacities exist?</li></ul>
What *resources* will be needed to deal with the problems?	<ul><li>What resources will affected communities require?</li><li>What resources are available or likely to become available?</li><li>What resources will need to be mobilized?</li></ul>

3. **Methodology:** How will you collect the data?

   - How will you decide which information to collect?

   - How will you carry out the assessment?

   - How much of the required information can be obtained by secondary data?

   - Which information sources will you use, and why?

   - What will your primary data needs be?

   - Which questionnaires, tools and checklists will you use?

   - Which sites will you select, and why?

   - Which individuals and groups will you consult, and why?

   - What assumptions will you make about the current or future situation?

4. **Analysis:** How will you analyse your data and present your findings?

   - How will you review secondary data (storage, combination, interpretation)?

   - How will you store and process primary data (database, comparison with secondary data, presenting preliminary findings)?

   - How will you validate your findings, is there a need to include other stakeholders?

   - What are your graphing and mapping needs for both analysis and reporting?

   - How should the findings be presented, reported and disseminated?

5. **Resources:** What do you need to implement the
    assessment? Work with the parts of your organization
    listed in **Tool 1** to mobilize the resources you need to
    implement the methodology successfully. The main
    focus of these resources will be your assessment
    team, who will carry out the assessment plan.

Tool 3: What skills and characteristics do my assessment team/working group need?

Table 6. What skills and characteristics do my assessment team/working group need?

☐ Experience in **qualitative**, participatory research methods
☐ Experience in emergency programming and project design
☐ Technical and sector expertise where necessary, such as WASH and food security
☐ Understanding of cross-cutting issues, such as gender and environment
☐ Language skills for the assessment area (include translators for team members who do not speak the language)
☐ Previous experience of similar disasters
☐ Experience in communications (for example, in dealing with the media for advocacy)
☐ Experience in data management and analysis (for example, in using software such as databases and analytical tools)
☐ Operational experience (for example, security, logistics, administration)
☐ Fundraising experience (for example, in talking to donors and writing proposals)
☐ Mix of **generalists** and specialists as needed
☐ Gender, age, and ethnic balance

(continued)

Table 6. What skills and characteristics do my assessment team/working group need? *(continued)*

☐ Representation of international, national, and local actors
☐ Objectivity and neutrality
☐ Good local knowledge (geographic and cultural), including access to local networks (it can be useful to include representatives of the population living in the affected area.)
☐ Willingness to live and work in difficult conditions

Tool 4: How do I train my assessment team?

Train all staff members working on the assessment. Training is required even if they have carried out assessments in the past. Include support staff, such as drivers and translators.

What do they need to learn?

- assessment plan overall;
- background, goal and objectives of the assessment;
- humanitarian principles and ethics in assessment;
- methodology and resourcing;
- assessment timeframe and geographical scope;
- team member roles and responsibilities;
- induction and briefing specific to each role;
- site and group selection process and guidance;
- primary data collection techniques to be used;
- communication skills for different groups, for example, older people;
- how to use the assessment tools, questionnaires, etc.;
- reporting requirements, including reporting lines;
- communications, security and emergency procedures;
- administrative and logistics arrangements; and
- how to use specific technology.

Check with colleagues to identify any other learning objectives.

Prepare a briefing package covering the pre-crisis and current situation. Distribute it before or during training, and use it for briefing other staff members, including new employees and visiting guests.

What should I include in the assessment briefing package?

- secondary data review;
- a map of the area;
- disaster summary sheets on the typical impacts of the specific disaster;
- guidelines on data collection techniques;
- instructions for site and group selection;
- list of key terms;
- logistics and movements brief (access, weather, etc.);
- social and cultural brief (beliefs, practices, etc., of affected populations);
- security and communications procedures; and
- details of emergency contacts and security procedures.

Check with colleagues to identify any other briefing material.

Tool 5: How can I give disaster-affected communities a voice?

The way you carry out the assessment will influence the whole relationship between your organization and the community. Your assessment must reflect community views in a useful and significant way. Community participation should not end with the assessment, it should continue for the whole of the project.

Table 7. Building community participation

Approach	Detail
Build an assessment team with the right composition and skills.	Ensure the team has gender, age and ethnic balance. Train members in community engagement and participatory skills.
Ensure community awareness of the assessment.	If possible, notify the local community and local authorities before the assessment. When you arrive, introduce your organization and team and explain the objectives, methodology and timeframe of the assessment.
Design the assessment and analysis plan to reflect priorities of affected populations, not just experts.	Ask communities to rank their priorities. Ensure the assessment considers issues like gender, violence, discrimination, and protection.

(continued)

Table 7. Building community participation *(continued)*

Approach	Detail
Encourage stake-holder support from the earliest opportunity.	Where possible, involve government officials, community leaders and other members of the community in planning and implementing the assessment.
Gather a wide range of views from the community through the people you choose as key informants and focus group participants.	Do not just talk to experts, government officials and community leaders, talk to ordinary members of the population. Interview men, women, boys and girls of different ages and backgrounds, particularly from vulnerable groups.
Avoid creating assessment fatigue in disaster-affected communities.	Share your plans and findings with other organizations and local authorities. Coordinate your assessment to avoid duplicating field visits. Consider joint assessments when appropriate.
Manage expecta-tions.	If assistance is urgently needed and you can provide it, do so during the assessment. However, do not make promises about future assistance that you cannot keep.

(continued)

Table 7. Building community participation *(continued)*

Do not put communities at unnecessary risk.	Include security and privacy of disaster-affected populations in your planning. Plan the assessment to include risk analysis for your team and the community.
Follow through on assessment findings and recommendations.	Explain any decisions made based on the assessment findings to the community using appropriate language.

Tool 6: How do I collect secondary data?

Reviewing secondary data can take a lot of time. You will need staff working only on gathering and analysing the data – this can be done remotely by experienced staff, saving time for in-country staff. Staff will need to have or be able to call on:

- general emergency programming skills;
- sector experience; and
- local knowledge of relevant geographic areas.

> **Box 5. What sorts of secondary baseline data might be available?**
>
> - population figures and demographics (for example, population breakdown by gender and age);
> - social and economic data (average household size, gender roles, livelihood practices);
> - scale and distribution of displaced populations;
> - details of pre-existing vulnerabilities;
> - **spatial data** (political/administrative boundaries, settlement locations);
> - health data (mortality and morbidity data);
> - food security and nutrition data;
> - access and availability of water;
> - hygiene and sanitation practices;
> - location and status of utilities (water, sanitation and power);

(continued)

Box 5. What sorts of secondary baseline data might be available? (continued)

- location and status of infrastructure (roads, health facilities and communications);
- disaster preparedness and contingency plans; and
- maps and satellite imagery.

Make clear in your assessment report when you use secondary data, and state your sources. However, some of your secondary data may be confidential or politically sensitive and the source should not be revealed. In such cases you should clarify with the source if the data can be attributed, anonymised, or only used for analysis. Where no data is available, make this clear in your report so that others can follow up if necessary. Decide how accurate and useful the data is by checking it against the following questions:

- How was the data collected and analysed, and was it credible?
- Who is the source of the data? Are they reliable?
- When was the data collected? How relevant is it to the current situation?
- Is the data consistent with other independent sources that you have?
- Why was the data collected? Is there any bias in the data?

Potential sources for pre- and in-crisis secondary data are listed in Table 8. There are three types of secondary data sources:

- **Pre-crisis**: government and non-government organizations often collect data to support their work *before* a crisis. This **baseline data** can be used to identify problems, vulnerabilities and risks that existed before the disaster.

- **In-crisis**: when the disaster hits, the same organizations will start collecting data about the disaster. While this data is often not very accurate, it can be compared to pre-crisis data to assess the impact of the disaster.

- **Organizational learning**: many organizations (including yours) will have carried out evaluations and recorded lessons learned as part of their work. These documents can be valuable data sources. They can also give you tips and lessons on carrying out the assessment, including mistakes or assumptions that you should avoid.

Use your personal networks to get documents from a wide range of sources. Organizational learning documents are usually internal. To find them, ask your colleagues and people from other organizations (for example in **cluster** meetings) and look for online resources. Start by collecting data at the national level – particularly **quantitative** sources such as census, humanitarian profile, health and nutrition statistics, and demographic data. Then look for more detail by group, location or sector. Look for data that is **disaggregated** (for example, demographics broken down by gender and age) or detailed (for example, on the lowest level of administrative boundaries available). Use references in these documents to find other potential sources.

Table 8. Sources of secondary data

Source	Examples
National institutions	Government ministries, universities and research institutions, local authorities
United Nations agencies, international and national NGOs	Situation reports, assessment reports, cluster meeting minutes, funding appeals, humanitarian profiles, epidemiological profiles, disaster summary sheets
International and local media	Television reports, newspaper and magazine articles
Databases and datasets	EM-DAT, PreventionWeb, ALNAP Evaluative Reports Database, Common Operational Datasets
Geospatial data and satellite imagery	UNOSAT, Google Earth
Websites	ReliefWeb, Alertnet, Shelter Centre Library, DevInfo, UN country portals
Social media	Facebook, Twitter
Large-scale surveys	Demographic and Health Surveys (DHS), Multiple Indicator Cluster Surveys (MICS), censuses
Can you think of any other sources?	

Tool 7: How do I collect primary data?

Gathering primary data involves site selection, tool selection or design, field testing, and a range of data collection techniques.

In some assessments, too many sites are surveyed by teams with limited skills and experience, using questionnaires that are too detailed for the early phases of the disaster. The result is wasted effort, and a lot of unused information. It is more useful to use more experienced teams to collect data from a limited number of sites, using short questionnaires designed to capture information that is not available from secondary sources.

There are four constraints to site selection: time, access, security, and resources. You will not have the resources to visit everywhere in a disaster-affected area, so you will have to adopt a sampling strategy to ensure that your assessment is as useful as possible. A sampling strategy sets out a system for deciding how many sites to visit in which areas to collect primary data. The sample will be a cross-section of affected communities or groups (such as internally displaced people and host communities) in selected geographical areas.

Planning your data collection

The best approach in the first days and weeks after a crisis is **purposive sampling**. Purposive sampling means choosing your sample – i.e. where you will visit and who you will talk to – with a specific purpose or group(s) in mind. Purposive sampling is useful when you need to quickly reach a specific segment of the population and where sampling for proportionality is not the primary concern (**Tool 8**).

In the first two weeks after an emergency, it is more realistic to collect information at community level (for example, village or site), or at the group level (for example, internally displaced people, or resident population) than at household or individual level. The objective of a purposive sample is to identify if the crisis has affected different geographical areas or affected groups in the same way, or to see how needs differ or compare across them. However, remember that you cannot make conclusions about the entire affected population by looking at community-level information gathered through purposive sampling.

You need to **disaggregate** data by sex and age whenever possible (Box 6 gives a standard example of this) and to include questions that enable you to compare the needs of different groups – for example, women are likely to have different security concerns than men.

Do not just visit the worst-affected areas. If you do, you may over-estimate the impact of the disaster. Instead, aim to visit a range of sites that will provide

Box 6. Disaggregation by sex and age	
Male	**Female**
0-5 years	0-5 years
6-12	6-12
13-17	13-17
18-49	18-49
50-59	50-59

a better overview of community needs. For example, in case of a tropical storm, choose communities in coastal areas compared to further inland, urban vs rural areas, etc.

Plan your methodology before the assessment. Select the most appropriate collection methods to gather the data you require, and plan and test the tools you will use. Using a range of methods will strengthen your assessment, but only if the assessment team is capable of using those methods effectively. The simplest, most common methods are direct observation, key informant interviews, and community group discussions. These are briefly described below and Table 9 shows where you can find detailed guidance on these methods and on more advanced techniques.

Table 9. Guidance on data collection techniques

Method	Further guidance
Key informant interviews	IFRC 2008. *Guidelines for Assessment in Emergencies*, Chapter 6 *ACAPS Technical Brief - Direct Observation and Key Informant Interview Techniques*
Community group discussion	IFRC 2008. *Guidelines for Assessment in Emergencies*, Chapter 6
Direct observation	*ACAPS Technical Brief - Direct Observation and Key Informant Interview Techniques*

(continued)

Table 9. Guidance on data collection techniques
(continued)

Method	Further guidance
In case the affected geographical area is limited, and you have the necessary time, resources and skills, use participatory methods such as: • Daily calendars • Seasonal calendars • Transect walks • Historical timelines • Proportional piling • Pair-wise ranking • Why-why tree • Mapping exercises	ALNAP Participation Handbook IFRC 2008. *Guidelines for Assessment in Emergencies*, Chapter 7 *Groupe URD, Participation Handbook for Humanitarian Field Worker*s

Direct observation

What is direct observation?

Direct observation provides a snapshot of an affected location and adds context and meaning to data collected through interviews.

There are two types of observation:

1. Structured observation (*looking for*), where you look for a specific behaviour, object or event (or

its absence) – for example, whether people wash with soap before meals. A checklist is normally used to remind you of key issues and to record your observations.
2.   Unstructured observation (*looking at*), where you look to see what issues exist – for example, how women and men move in and out of a camp. A short set of open-ended questions is normally used that are answered by the observers.

How should observation be organized?

The observers are briefed. They decide which site(s) will be observed, what things they will look for and how to record these observations. Multiple observers can be used to gather different views and interpretations.

What should the observer do?

The observer explains why they want to observe people at the site, asks permission from the people living there, and explains how the information collected will be used. Invite people living at the site to join the observation. Observe with an open mind. If feasible, compare the key informant interviews as much as possible. Respect local culture and gender dynamics: dress, behave, and communicate respectfully. Be sensitive to local concerns and the impact of the crisis.

What happens during observation?

Start with a walk around the location with one or two community members. Ask them questions about what you observe on the way, to explain what has happened, and why things are as they are.

Table 10. Why use direct observation?

Advantages	Disadvantages
• Can be used to rapidly collect different types of information in an emergency. • Does not require many resources to implement. • Does not necessarily require much training for staff. • Can be used to cross-check informant responses and other assessment methods. • Can generate questions for further assessments. • Gives assessment teams their own perspective.	• Provides only a snapshot, not a complete picture. • Is of limited use in a quickly changing situation. • Provides only partial information about community capacities and priorities. • Requires technical expertise of observers to answer questions. • Subjective perceptions can affect observation and distort findings. • May affect observed people's behaviour and distort findings.

Make diversions to visit locations of specific interest, such as water collection points, latrines, communal washing areas, schools, storage facilities, grave sites, markets, and health facilities. Observations are recorded immediately to ensure that they are accurate and reliable.

If there are multiple observers, they compare their notes and discuss their observations as soon as possible.

Key informant interviews

What is a key informant interview?

A key informant interview is a structured or unstructured conversation with a selected individual. A key informant interview occurs when an individual with prior knowledge of the affected community is questioned to gather information on the consequences and effects of the crisis and ensuing community needs. Key informants provide the field team with their impressions on behalf of the community. This information creates a shared impression of the community's perspective as to the impact of the crisis and humanitarian concerns. Characteristics of key informants are that they are well versed on their communities, its inhabitants, the site visited, and/or the crisis, because of professional background, leadership role, or personal experience.

Why use key informant interviews?

Key informant interviews are conducted to obtain general information about the population (for example, from a camp manager, local authorities, mayor) or technical information from people representing specific professions, for example, health workers or school teachers. A key informant interview is cost-effective (time, financial, human resources) in comparison to a household survey.

There are two types of interviews, each of which has a different approach and different advantages (Table 11).

Table 11. Semi-structured and structured interviews

Semi-structured	Structured
HOW? Uses a checklist of open-ended questions in conversation to stimulate discussion on specific topics.	**HOW?** Uses a questionnaire on selected topics to ensure that all interviews address the same issues in the same way.
WHY? Analysing interviews is labour-intensive since the conversation may be quite wide-ranging, but answers can be summarised around main points and then placed into categories to show respondents' priorities. Summary sheets can then be aggregated and compared to identify patterns and priorities.	**WHY?** Structure makes it easier to aggregate and compare answers with more precision than semi-structured interviews. Designing the questionnaire requires expertise and experience. Informant selection is critical, and carrying out the interviews can be labour-intensive.

It is recommended to use semi-structured interview when you want to capture information that cannot be pre-coded in a questionnaire, or when you need contextual information to better understand perceptions.

How should the interview be organized?

Interviewers decide in advance who they will interview, what questions they will ask, how they will ask them, and how to record the answers. They brief community leaders and ask for permission to conduct the interviews.

Try to interview several key informants in each location to cross-check information. Prioritize interviews with vulnerable or marginalized individuals. Do the interviews at times and places that are safe and convenient for assessment team members and informants. They should last as long as is convenient for the informant, but try not to exceed 45 minutes to an hour for each interview. A good interpreter should be available if necessary. Where possible, assessment team members should meet halfway through the field visit to discuss progress and agree any necessary changes to the approach or timing. Team members can also share initial findings, share challenges, and note gaps in information. This enables their fellow team members to examine these issues during the second half of the field visit.

What should the interviewer do?

The interviewer asks the informant for permission to carry out the interview and makes sure that the informant understands why the interview is happening, and what will happen with the information from the interview. Doing key informant interviews requires good interviewing skills. Spend time establishing a good rapport with the person you interview before you go into specific questions. A good relationship between the interviewer and the interviewee goes a long way in getting good quality data. Take notes throughout the interview and ensure that the information is transferred safely and without distortion. Make sure you do not become too focused on the questionnaire or form you are using. Remember that a key informant interview is more than a survey, and constant note-taking may destroy the flow of the interview. Ideally, two of you should be conducting the interview, so one can take notes and the other keep the conversation going.

What happens during the interview?

The interview should start with factual questions that are simple to answer. It should move on to more sensitive issues only if this is appropriate and only when the informant is relaxed. Use findings from direct observation to verify information and unpick inconsistencies in key informant responses. Triangulate information from multiple key informants during the interview, and refine questions for future key informants based on inconsistent or missing information. Be aware of both your biases and those of the key informant and how they might affect results.

The interviewer should be aware of potential negative impacts on the key informant if the questions are about sensitive topics such as **gender-based violence**. At the end, the interviewer thanks the informant for their participation, and asks for permission to use their names (if relevant).

Community group discussions

What is a community group discussion?

It is a method that can be used to gather information from a group of people who are invited to participate in a structured discussion on specific topics with the help of an experienced facilitator. Ideally, the group should be small enough to maintain focus, give everybody a chance to speak, and allow individuals to address the group as a whole. A group of four to eight persons is an ideal size for a community group discussion. Groups smaller than this are more accurately seen as multiple key informant groups and larger groups can be difficult to manage.

However, following a crisis, large groups of people may live in close confines and being rigorous about group size or composition may be difficult. Bear in mind that a community group discussion is a flexible tool that has been developed for rapid information gathering and it is different from other established social research methods. Group size and structure should be determined based on the context and this should be clearly documented in the methodology section of the assessment findings.

Why use community group discussions?

Community groups enable you to gather information and perspectives that may not be possible through other data collection techniques. Community groups enable alternative perspectives and allow for greater diversity. Unlike the one-way flow of information in an interview, community group discussions generate data through group discussion and can result in a conclusion collectively owned by the group. Listening as people share and compare their different points of view provides a wealth of information, not just about what they think, but why they perceive the situation the way they do. The discussion's aim is to provide an understanding of how the disaster is affecting a community, from the perspective of the community.

How should the discussion be organized?

A community group discussion needs to be thoroughly planned before moving to the field. Important questions when planning include:

- How many sites should be visited (**Tool 8**)?
- What defines a site? Is it determined geographically as a specific location, or is it determined by other factors such as living arrangements? For example, spontaneous settlements, organized camps, damaged own houses, or host families? Organizing discussion groups by criteria such as living arrangements can help compare across the different groups when analysing the data.
- How many community group discussions should we aim for?
- Will the discussion be limited to one community group per site?
- Can male and female community members be included in the same community group discussion, or will better quality information be achieved through separate male and female discussions?

Remember that once a structure for community group discussions in the particular field trip is decided, one needs to be consistent across sites. Having mixed groups in one location requires a similar setup in the next to allow for appropriate comparison across population groups and geographical locations.

The participants are usually selected on site, generally ad hoc, but as far as possible, each group should contain a mix of individuals from different backgrounds, responsibilities, genders, ages, and religious and/or ethnic minorities to ensure a full picture of the affected site. The selection of the participants will also depend on the specific interest, aims and objectives of the assessment.

An assessment covering multiple sectors can take a long time. The group should meet in a place where they can carry out the discussion, preferably sitting comfortably in a circle. The assessment team/facilitators should be aware of any real or perceived negative consequences that may be felt by community members from sharing information openly. Where possible try to avoid the presence of leaders or other authority figures as they can dominate the discussion and prevent other participants from speaking. Use them as key informants instead.

What should the facilitator do?

Experience has shown that it is useful to have two facilitators for each community group discussion; one note-taker and one facilitator. Ensure that the facilitators are of appropriate age and gender so that, where culturally required, male groups are facilitated by men and female groups by women. The facilitators should have the appropriate language skills and cultural knowledge to communicate with the community. Facilitators with experience in working with communities are desirable; however this may not always be possible. It is therefore important to have a facilitator who has been thoroughly briefed on the format of the discussion. The facilitator should be skilled at managing group discussions, gauging the agreement or disagreement of the overall group with what is being said, balancing dominant personalities, addressing potentially tricky and/or upsetting questions, and be well versed in the topics that are being covered.

Familiarity with the assessment tool being used is vital so definitions and discussion approach is used as consistently as possible across the assessment teams. The facilitator should establish ground rules (for example, everyone has a right to speak, no one person has the right answer, and speakers should not be interrupted), ensure that everybody understands the purpose of the discussion, and get permission from the group to take notes. Effective interview techniques require skill in four key areas: listening, paraphrasing, probing, and note taking.

What happens during the discussion?

The facilitator should use a questionnaire or an agreed set of questions to stimulate and focus discussion. To achieve rapid consolidation and analysis of findings, a tool that has predefined responses based on lessons learned and knowledge of the situation is useful. However, this should not be used to limit the inclusion of new and unforeseen responses from the group. Include some open-ended questions allowing for multiple possible replies, but avoid leading questions that suggest the facilitator's opinion or a preferred answer.

Reaching consensus is important. Questions may allow one single response, multiple responses or they may require a prioritization of responses (for example, first, second and third priorities). If there are vastly varied responses, achieving this consensus will require very clear definitions and skilled management of the discussion. There may be times where noting 'no clear consensus' will be relevant, and recording the range of opinions will be required.

Tool 8: How do I select affected sites and vulnerable groups?

Tool 7 identified **purposive sampling** as the best selection approach in the early phases of a response. But how should you select specific sites to visit and groups to talk to? Based on your secondary data review and consultation with other organizations (especially those with coordination responsibilities, such as **cluster** leads), you can use the questions in the Table 12 to select sites. When you answer these questions, mark

Table 12. Selection of sampling sites

Question	Focus questions
Where is the greatest impact of the disaster?	• Which areas are usually the most vulnerable? • Which areas are reported to be most affected?
Where is the greatest need?	Which areas have the least capacity?
Where is the least assistance?	• Which areas are receiving the least assistance? • Which areas already receive support from other organizations?
In which locations can you have the most impact?	• In which areas does your organization already have capacity? • In which areas can you build capacity or start new work?

out the locations on maps showing the affected area and specific locations in the affected area.

Once you have selected sites, you need to select individuals and groups to talk with at those sites. Table 13 gives examples of issues that contribute to **vulnerability** and of groups that might be affected by those issues. Do not assume that the perspective of one member of a group reflects the views of the whole group. Remember that many issues are closely linked, (for example, lack of land tenure and environmental degradation often go hand-in-hand), and individuals can belong to more than one group.

Table 13. Selection of interviewees

Issue	Example
Discrimination/ marginalization	Women and girls
Displacement	Displaced in public buildings or camps
Social isolation	Older people and disabled people
Environmental degradation	Communities on marginal land
Climate variability	Communities in coastal areas
Poverty	Low-income groups
Lack of land tenure	Displaced communities; slum residents
Poor governance	Low-status groups
Ethnicity	Minority groups
Class or caste	Minority groups
Religious or political affiliation	Minority groups

Tool 9: How do I organize a field visit?

Table 14. Are you ready for the field visit?

Question	Suggestion
Have you clearly identified which affected areas your team will visit?	Use a map to mark the areas for your team.
Is there enough time to carry out the assessment properly?	Use a calendar to identify key dates in the assessment cycle.
Have you reviewed any lessons learned, evaluations or other documents available for that area or the particular type of disaster?	Use secondary data, including personal contacts and online databases, to gather relevant data and documents (**Tool 6**).
Have you collated any background or baseline data that you have on the area and the affected populations?	
Have you selected an assessment team with the right balance of skills and backgrounds for that area and the affected communities?	Use the checklist from **Tool 3**. What skills and characteristics do my assessment team need?

(continued)

Table 14. Are you ready for the field visit? *(continued)*

Question	Suggestion
Have you clearly defined individual roles, responsibilities and reporting lines within the assessment team?	Prepare a one-page sheet that lists all the members of the team and a short paragraph describing their role.
Have you checked that all team members are familiar with the assessment methodology and tool?	Carry out a one-day training session to make sure that all staff use the methodology correctly (**Tool 4**).
Have you made sure that all of your team members are clear about the overall objectives of their visit?	Hold a team briefing before each visit, and raise any specific issues the team needs to be aware of (**Tool 4**).
Have you taken care of all the administrative and logistical issues for the trip?	Make sure that you get any permissions necessary for the visit, from the government or from the community. Book all transport and accommodation in advance. Decide whether you need separate living quarters for men and women in the team.
Is your field trip coordinated with any government or non-government stakeholders?	Inform government officials, local authorities and other field actors of the date and location of your assessment.

(continued)

Table 14. Are you ready for the field visit? *(continued)*

Question	Suggestion
Have you checked conditions in the area for:	
Transport?	Check the latest reports from other organizations. Ask local staff.
Weather?	Check the latest weather forecasts and seasonal trends. Ask local staff.
Security?	Check security briefs and levels (including government and UN). Brief assessment team members on the security situation and any standard operating procedures.

Table 15. What happens during the field visit?

Question	Suggestion
Have you planned each day?	Prepare for the day's work the evening before. This will include deciding which location(s) will be visited; drawing up checklists of the main information required; agreeing on the ways the information will be collected (these can be changed during the day); and defining responsibilities for who will do what on that day.

(continued)

Table 15. What happens during the field visit?
(continued)

Question	Suggestion
Have you talked with the local authorities (both government and community)?	Talk to the local authorities and community leaders when you arrive. Explain who you are, why you are visiting, and how you are going to collect data. If necessary, ask for permission to carry out the assessment. You may prepare and distribute a sheet describing your organization, explaining the assessment and providing contact details.
Are you using observation techniques?	Take an informal walk around the area accompanied by local people to get an impression of the community. Even if you are not using direct observation techniques, observe everything around you during the assessment.
Are you interviewing people?	Identify individuals (key informants) and groups (community groups) to talk to.
Have you organized daily team meetings?	Hold regular team meetings for members to share impressions and ideas. Identify and address challenges, agree any changes to the schedule and provide support to each other.

(continued)

Table 15. What happens during the field visit?
(continued)

Question	Suggestion
Have you organized community meetings during or after the visit?	Hold meetings with community representatives when the assessment is complete. Explain what you have done and what you plan to do, but do not make any commitments regarding future assistance.
Are you maintaining good communications?	The team must keep regular contact with their coordinator and/or support office according to an agreed communications schedule. The location of assessment team members must be known at all times, and any problems with communications equipment must be reported immediately.
Are you identifying issues for follow-up?	Keep a separate file in which you can keep notes on critical issues that require more attention, particularly gaps in the assessment, or immediate assistance.
Can you think of anything else?	

Tool 10: What support does my assessment team need?

Make sure your assessment team has the support it needs. Be clear about who is responsible for providing that support. Each member of the assessment team must also take responsibility for their own safety and security.

Table 16. Support requirements for assessment teams

Security	☐ Is there a security plan?
	☐ Do the transport plan, communications schedule and other administrative requirements (see below) support the security plan?
	☐ Has the team received security clearance from your organization, national authorities and any others that may demand it, for example, armed groups?
Transport	☐ Is there a transport plan?
	☐ Are transport arrangements confirmed for the whole assessment? Are there back-up transport options available?
	☐ Does your transport have the necessary safety equipment? Do your team members know where it is and how to use it?

(continued)

Table 16. Support requirements for assessment teams *(continued)*

Communications	☐ Is there a communications schedule agreed between the head office and the assessment team?
	☐ Does your team have the necessary communications equipment (including back-up options)? Do they know how to use it properly?
	☐ Do all assessment team members have phone numbers to call in a crisis?
Accommodation and meals	☐ Has accommodation been confirmed for the team?
	☐ Have gender-sensitive considerations been made for accommodation?
	☐ Will meals be available for the team during the assessment? If not, have you provided supplies?
Cash and administration	☐ Does the team have enough cash?
	☐ Is it clear who will manage cash and expenses?
	☐ Do you have security measures to ensure safe cash handling?

(continued)

Table 16. Support requirements for assessment teams
(continued)

Visas and travel permissions	☐ Do all team members have visas, support letters or any other forms required to enter the country or region? ☐ Does the team have necessary travel permissions/documentation to travel to and in disaster-affected areas (including any restricted areas)? ☐ Do the travel permissions cover the vehicles the team will be using?
Insurance	☐ Do all team members (national and international) have insurance? ☐ Has the insurance company been notified about the assessment?
Interpreters	☐ Do you have enough interpreters to support the team? ☐ Do you have enough female interpreters for interviewing women? ☐ Have the interpreters been trained and tested?
Equipment	☐ Has the team been provided with the necessary equipment? Check using **Tool 11**.

Tool 11: What equipment does my assessment team need?

Table 17. Equipment required for assessment team

For each person	☐ Organizational and national identification card
	☐ Insurance and emergency contact details
	☐ Laptop / tablet computer / smartphone (as needed)
	☐ Mobile phone (plus charger, SIM card and prepaid credits)
	☐ Emergency camping supplies (tents, bedding, torch and spare battery, etc.)
	☐ USB memory stick
	☐ Copies of assessment guides and data collection forms (key informant, direct observation, focus group)
	☐ Other materials for participatory techniques (flip-chart sheets, felt-tip pens, seasonal calendar formats)
	☐ Other stationery (paper, clipboard, notebooks, rulers, pens, pencils, sharpeners, erasers, stapler and staples)
	☐ Calculator
	☐ Cashbox

(continued)

Table 17. Equipment required for assessment team
(continued)

For each vehicle (maintained, serviced and equipped)	☐ 2 spare wheels and jack
	☐ Pull rope and shovel
	☐ 1 fire extinguisher
	☐ 1 large first aid kit
	☐ 1 small toolkit
	☐ 1 jerry can (spare fuel)
	☐ Paperwork (including insurance)
For each team	☐ Laptops / tablet computers / smartphones (as needed)
	☐ 2 satellite telephones
	☐ 2 radio handsets
	☐ 1 GPS unit
	☐ 1 mobile internet-dongle
	☐ 1 portable printer, paper and spare ink
	☐ Food and drinking water for one day for full team
	☐ Maps of selected locations
	☐ Visibility material (t-shirts, flags, stickers)
	☐ Mosquito nets and insect repellent
	☐ Spare batteries and chargers for all devices
	☐ Spare copies of Sphere and other standards

Tool 12: What technology should I use?

Information and communication technologies, such as the internet and mobile phones, have changed how our organizations work, how we engage with disaster-affected communities, and how we collect, analyse and share data.

> **Box 7. What can technology help with?**
>
> - **Coverage**, for example, better maps and satellite imagery for planning field visits;
> - **Speed**, for example, less time to process data using digital information management systems (such as databases);
> - **Integrity**, for example, entering data directly via handheld devices preventing the errors that happen in moving data from paper to computer;
> - **Analytical** capacity, for example, using geographic information systems (GIS) to manage spatial data; and
> - **Robustness**, for example, storing data in a remote database to provide more security.

You need to carefully plan and manage the use of technology in an assessment. You do not have to be an expert but you should understand what the technology can and cannot do, what it will cost in time and money, and whether it fits well with the work you do. We should be aware of the tendency to gravitate towards new, fancy solutions. It is easy to become blinded by their novelty, potentially overlooking their actual usefulness. New tools could potentially give data and subsequent information products a false sense of quality and accuracy. Bear in mind that the quality of the information rests on the quality of the data and not on the way it is processed or presented.

- Choose the most suitable technology for your activities – do not just use the newest technology.
- Check the claims made by technology staff, including those in your own organization.
- Find out how much the technology will cost your organization – not just in money but also in the time it will take to introduce successfully.
- Make sure the solutions are relevant. A well-functioning information management process is not an end in itself, but just an important stepping-stone in the decision-making process. Technological solutions should be introduced and applied with this in mind.
- Adopt new technology and train your staff in how to use it *before* an emergency. Doing this in the middle of an emergency is likely to lead to failure and waste resources.
- During assessments, provide technical support to your team to make sure that the technology works as planned.
- Make sure your technological solution is resilient and able to withstand the austere working environment often found in humanitarian crises. It also needs to be able to withstand the often less than gentle treatment it may receive from technically inexperienced staff.

- After the assessment, get feedback on the implementation.
- Do not forget that low technology is readily available – pen and paper always works!

Table 18 will help you decide whether a new technology is suitable for you.

Table 18. Technology checklist

☐ How complex is the technology? How hard is it to use? Do people need training to use it? The more time and money it takes to set it up, the harder it will be to implement.
☐ How suitable is the technology for your organization? Can it be easily included in your workflow? Could it become an obstacle and increase an already packed workload rather than supporting more efficient work processes?
☐ What are the needs of your assessment team? Do your staff really need this technology? If they can work nearly as effectively without it, then it may not be worth getting.
☐ Does it add value to the response and optimize existing solutions? Technology should be 'need to have' and not just something that is 'nice to have' – especially not if there is a simpler solution already available.
☐ Is the solution able to function when standing alone, or does it need further technology to function properly?
☐ What is the capacity of your assessment team? If they have this technology, will they be able to use it? It may bring unexpected costs on things like training.

(continued)

Table 18. Technology checklist *(continued)*

☐ What is the local operating environment like? Is this technology suitable for where you work? For example, working environments that suffer from power cuts may make it hard to use.
☐ Is technical support available? Is there anybody who can fix it, if things go wrong? Without support, any failure in the middle of the assessment could be disastrous.

Tool 13: How can I ensure a high-quality assessment?

Be accountable

Accountability should be at the heart of the assessment, no matter how hard this may be in the early stages. You are accountable for the quality of the assessment to your organization and to the communities that you are assessing. *Accountability and Impact Measurement: The Good Enough Guide* has information to help you do your job accountably.

Use key indicators, standards and guidelines

- Use the *Sphere for Assessments* guide for key indicators of a good assessment.
- Use humanitarian community standards and guidelines for assessing specific sectors.

Table 19. Resources to help you assess specific sectors (for full reference details see 'Standards and guidance' section p.97)

Sector	Resource
Water supply, sanitation and hygiene promotion (WASH)	*The Sphere Handbook* (The Sphere Project, 2011) pp79–138

(continued)

Table 19. Resources to help you assess specific sectors
(continued)

Sector	Resource
Food security and nutrition	*The Sphere Handbook* (The Sphere Project, 2011) pp139–238 *Emergency Food Security Assessment Handbook* (World Food Programme, 2009)
Shelter, settlement and non-food items	*The Sphere Handbook* (The Sphere Project, 2011) pp239–86 *Local Estimate of Needs for Shelter and Settlement* Field Version (UN-Habitat, 2009)
Health action	*The Sphere Handbook* (The Sphere Project, 2011) pp287–354
Protection	*The Sphere Handbook* (The Sphere Project, 2011) pp25–48 *Rapid Protection Assessment Toolkit* (Global Protection Cluster, 2012)
Education	INEE *Minimum Standards for Education* (INEE, 2010) *The Short Guide to Rapid Education Joint Needs Assessments* (Global Education Cluster, 2010)
Livestock	*Livestock Emergency Guidelines and Standards* (LEGS, 2009)
Economic recovery	*Minimum Economic Recovery Standards* (The SEEP Network, 2013)
Camp management	*The Camp Management Toolkit* (Norwegian Refugee Council, 2008)

(continued)

Table 19. Resources to help you assess specific sectors
(continued)

Sector	Resource
Markets	*Market Analysis in Emergencies* (Sivakumaran, 2011)
Environment	*Framework for Assessing, Monitoring and Evaluating the Environment in Refugee-related Operations* (FRAME) (UNHCR and CARE, 2005)
Sex and age	*Sex and Age Matter* (Mazurana et al., 2011)
Mental health / psychosocial	*IASC Guidelines on Mental Health and Psychosocial Support in Emergency Settings* (IASC, 2007) *Humanitarian Emergency Settings Perceived Needs Scale* (HESPER) (WHO and King's College, 2011)
Other	

Prepare for the next assessment

If your organization did not have assessment procedures or contingency plans including provisions for assessments, develop them so that you are ready for the next emergency.

If your organization does have assessment procedures, improve them for the next emergency by adding any lessons identified.

Tool 14: How should I share my assessment findings?

1. Think about the different audiences who will use your findings

External	<ul><li>disaster-affected communities;</li><li>local and national authorities;</li><li>partners you work with;</li><li>**clusters** or other coordination meetings;</li><li>UN and other international agencies;</li><li>donors;</li><li>media organizations;</li><li>people in other humanitarian organizations; and</li><li>other assessment teams.</li></ul>
Internal	<ul><li>senior management team;</li><li>regional/global offices;</li><li>technical advisors; and</li><li>the next person in your job.</li></ul>
Any others?	

2. Think about which formats will be useful for your audience

- assessment report;
- situation report;
- powerpoint presentation;

- briefing note;
- verbal briefing;
- maps, infographics;
- graphs, charts and other visual aids; and
- *any others?*

3. Think about the different methods you can use to share them

- email;
- fax;
- one-to-one discussions;
- coordination meetings;
- teleconferences;
- hard copy distribution;
- web posting;
- presentations; and
- *any others?*

Tool 15: What should I put in my assessment report?

Table 20. Structure of the assessment report

Section	Contains
Author details	Name, date, organization, office
Executive summary	A brief and readable summary of the entire report
Assessment plan	• Goal and objectives • Terms of reference • Assessment team composition
Methodology	• Methods and approaches • Timeframe • Locations visited • Reason for chosen approach • Assumptions made for the assessment • Limitations of the assessment • Information gaps and requirements for further assessment
Background	• Context (social, economic, cultural, political) • Brief description of disaster and disaster area • Impact summary (physical, social, environmental, economic, political)

(continued)

Table 20. Structure of the assessment report *(continued)*

Section	Contains
General humanitarian situation	• **Drivers** of the crisis and underlying factors • Scope of the crisis and humanitarian profile • Status of populations living in affected areas (based on agreed humanitarian standards, such as Sphere) • National capacities and response • International capacities and response • Humanitarian access • Coverage and gaps • Key priorities
Overview	Key issues such as displacement patterns, epidemiological information, and demographics
Technical sectors	Shelter, WASH, health, food security, etc.
Cross-cutting issues	Gender, environment, protection, disaster risk reduction, etc.
Response by other actors / Stakeholder analysis	Community, government (national and local), NGOs (national and international), UN agencies, donors, military, and other actors
Partnerships	• Current and proposed partnerships • Critical issues

(continued)

Table 20. Structure of the assessment report *(continued)*

Section	Contains
Operating conditions	• Security (including civil-military relations) • Logistics (including infrastructure damage) • Market conditions (including local availability of relief items) • Infrastructure conditions (for your own organization, for example, offices) • Government regulations and requirements for operations
Key findings	A summary of the analysis
Scenarios	Possible course of events that could occur based on informed assumptions, which may form the basis for humanitarian contingency planning
Recommendations	• Priority needs and proposed responses (short-term and mid-term) • Information gaps and future assessment needs
Annexes	Any additional information needed to understand the assessment

In some organizations, you may also be required to analyse and make recommendations in the following areas:

- management requirements;
- supply chain management / procurement / logistics;
- finance, administration and human resources management;
- information and communications technology (includes radio);
- media, donor relations, and fundraising; and
- information management and technology.

For each of these, you may need to consider:

- analysis of context / key issues;
- proposed approach;
- management structure;
- staffing requirements;
- roles and responsibilities;
- other resource requirements (equipment, supplies, etc.);
- budget;
- next steps and critical timings; and
- timeframe (from start-up to longer term).

RESOURCES AND GLOSSARY

Key resources

ACAPS (2011) *Technical Brief: Direct Observation and Key Informant Interview Techniques* ACAPS. Geneva, Switzerland.

ACAPS (2011) *Technical Brief: Purposive Sampling and Site Selection.* ACAPS. Geneva, Switzerland.

ACAPS (2012) *Desk Review: Rapid Estimation of Affected Population Figures.* ACAPS. Geneva, Switzerland.

ACAPS (2012) *Qualitative and Quantitative Research Techniques for Humanitarian Needs Assessment: An Introductory Brief.* ACAPS. Geneva, Switzerland.

ACAPS (2012) *Rapid Estimation of Affected Population Figures: Desk Review.* ACAPS. Geneva, Switzerland.

ACAPS (2012) *Technical Brief: Building an Effective Assessment Team.* ACAPS. Geneva, Switzerland.

ACAPS (2012) *Technical Brief: Coordinated Assessments in Emergencies. What We Know Now:*

http://dx.doi.org/10.3362/9781780448626.004

Key Lessons from Field Experience. ACAPS. Geneva, Switzerland.

ACAPS (2012) *Technical Brief: Scenario Building.* ACAPS. Geneva, Switzerland.

ACAPS (2013) *How to Approach a Dataset: Part 1 – 3 (Database Design, Data Preparation, and Analysis).* ACAPS. Geneva, Switzerland.

ACAPS (2013) *Severity and Priority – Their Measurement in Rapid Needs Assessments.* ACAPS. Geneva, Switzerland.

ACAPS (2013)*Technical Brief: Compared to What: Analytical Thinking and Needs Assessment.* ACAPS. Geneva, Switzerland.

ACAPS (2014) *Composite Measures of Local Disaster Impact – Lessons from Typhoon Yolanda, Philippines.* ACAPS. Geneva, Switzerland.

ACAPS (2014) *Technical Brief: Secondary Data Review – Sudden Onset Natural Disasters.* ACAPS. Geneva, Switzerland.

ACAPS and CDAC (2014) *Assessing Information and Communication Needs.* ACAPS/CDAC. Geneva, Switzerland.

ACAPS and the ECB Project (2011) *Joint Needs Assessment Bangladesh – Lessons Learned and Way Forward.* Emergency Capacity Building Project. Geneva, Switzerland.

Assessment and Classification of Emergencies (ACE) Project (2009) *Mapping of Key Emergency Needs Assessment and Analysis Initiatives.* UN OCHA. Geneva, Switzerland.

ALNAP (2003) *Participation by Crisis-Affected Populations in Humanitarian Action: A Handbook for Practitioners.* Overseas Development Institute. London, UK.

Brown, D., Donini, A. and Knox Clarke, P. (2014) *Engagement of Crisis-affected People in Humanitarian Action.* 29th ALNAP Annual Meeting, Overseas Development Institute. London, UK.

CARE (2009) *CARE Emergency Toolkit: Assessment.* CARE International. Geneva, Switzerland.

CDA Collaborative Learning Projects (2004) *The Do No Harm Handbook: The Framework for Analyzing the Impact of Assistance on Conflict.* Collaborative for Development Action, Inc. and CDA Collaborative Learning Projects. Cambridge MA, USA.

Conflict Sensitivity Consortium (2012) *How to Guide to Conflict Sensitivity.* Conflict Sensitivity Consortium. London, UK.

Darcy, J. and Hofmann, C.-A. (2003) *According to Need? Needs Assessment and Decision-Making in the Humanitarian Sector.* HPG Report 15, Overseas Development Institute. London, UK.

Dummett, C., Hagens, C. and Morel D. (2013) *Guidance on Participatory Assessments.* Catholic Relief Services. Baltimore MD, USA.

ECHO (2010) *Initial Needs Assessment Checklist (INAC)* Version 18/06/10. ECHO. Brussels, Belgium.

Emergency Capacity Building Project (2007) *Impact Measurement and Accountability in Emergencies: The Good Enough Guide.* Emergency Capacity Building

Project. Geneva, Switzerland. Project and Oxfam GB. Oxford, UK. Available from Practical Action Publishing, Rugby, UK.

Emergency Capacity Building Project (2013) *Emergency Food Security and Livelihoods 48 Hour Assessment Tool* Version 2, ECB and Oxfam GB. Oxford, UK.

Featherstone, A. (2011) *Strength in Numbers: Global Mapping Review of NGO Engagement in Coordinated Assessments.* Emergency Capacity Building Project. Geneva, Switzerland.

Garfield, R. with Blake, C., Chataigner, P. and Walton-Ellery, S. (2011) *Common Needs Assessments and Humanitarian Action.* HPN Network Paper 69, Overseas Development Institute. London, UK.

Global Education Cluster (2010) *The Short Guide to Rapid Joint Education Needs Assessments.* Unicef and Save the Children. Geneva, Switzerland.

Global Protection Cluster (2012) *Rapid Protection Assessment Toolkit* Version 5. Global Protection Cluster. Geneva, Switzerland.

Gonzalez, B.A., (2012) *Ensuring Inclusion of Older People in Initial Emergency Needs Assessments.* HelpAge International. London, UK.

Groupe URD *Participation Handbook for Humanitarian Field Workers.* Groupe URD. France. http://www.urd.org/Participation-Handbook

Hofmann, C.-A., Roberts, L., Shoham, J. and Harvey, P. (2004) *Measuring the Impact of Humanitarian*

Aid: A Review of Current Practice. HPG Report 17, Overseas Development Institute. London, UK.

IASC Emergency Shelter Cluster (2006) *Guidelines for Assessment in Emergencies.* UNHCR. IASC Needs Assessment Task Force. Geneva, Switzerland.

Inter-Agency Standing Committee (IASC) (2012) *Multi-Cluster/Sector Initial Rapid Assessment (MIRA).* IASC Needs Assessment Task Force. Geneva, Switzerland.

Inter-Agency Standing Committee (IASC) (2012) *Operational Guidance Note for Coordinated Assessments in Humanitarian Crises.* IASC Needs Assessment Task Force. Geneva, Switzerland.

IASC Sub-Working Group on Gender in Humanitarian Action (2005) *Guidelines for Gender-based Violence Interventions in Humanitarian Settings.* IASC Needs Assessment Task Force. Geneva, Switzerland.

International Committee of the Red Cross (ICRC) and International Federation of Red Cross and Red Crescent Societies (IFRC) (2008) *Guidelines for Assessment in Emergencies.* ICRC/IFRC. Geneva, Switzerland.

International Organization for Migration (2010) *IOM Data Protection Manual.* IOM. Geneva, Switzerland.

Mazurana, D., Benelli, P., Gupta, H. and Walker, P. (2011) *Sex and Age Matter: Improving Humanitarian Response in Emergencies.* Feinstein International Center, Tufts University, Boston MA, USA.

Planitz, A. (1997, updated 1999) *A Guide to Successful Damage and Needs Assessment.* South Pacific Disaster Reduction Programme. Suva, Fiji.

ReliefWeb (2008) *Glossary of Humanitarian Terms*. UN OCHA. Geneva, Switzerland.

Slim, H. and Bonwick, A. (2005) *Protection: An ALNAP Guide for Humanitarian Agencies*. Overseas Development Institute. London, UK.

The Sphere Project (2014) *Sphere for Assessments*. The Sphere Project. Geneva, Switzerland.

UNDAC (2013) *UNDAC Handbook*. UN OCHA. Geneva, Switzerland.

UN-Habitat (2009) *LENSS Tool Kit: Local Estimate of Needs for Shelter and Settlement: Field Version*. UN-HABITAT. Geneva, Switzerland.

UNHCR and CARE (2005) *Framework for Assessing, Monitoring and Evaluating the Environment in Refugee-related Operations (FRAME)*. UNHCR/CARE. Geneva, Switzerland.

US Agency for International Development, Bureau for Humanitarian Response, Office of Foreign Disaster Assistance (2005) *Field Operations Guide for Disaster Assessment and Response* (version 3.0). USAID. Washington DC, USA.

Watkins, R., Meiers, M.W. and Visser, Y. (2011) *A Guide to Assessing Needs: Essential Tools for Collecting Information, Making Decisions, and Achieving Development Results*. International Bank for Reconstruction and Development / International Development Association. Washington DC, USA.

Wigley, B. (2013) *Accountability to Affected Populations (AAP) and Communicating with*

Communities (CwC) Assessment Questions. Emergency Capacity Building Project. Geneva, Switzerland.

World Food Programme (WFP) (2009) Emergency Food Security Assessment Handbook (second edition). WFP. Rome, Italy.

WFP Emergency Needs Assessment Service (2009) Emergency Food Security Assessments: Technical Guidance Sheet No. 8: Introduction to Qualitative Data and Methods for Collection and Analysis in Food Security Assessments. WFP. Rome, Italy.

World Health Organization and King's College London (2011) The Humanitarian Emergency Settings Perceived Needs Scale (HESPER): Manual with Scale. WHO. Geneva, Switzerland and London, UK.

Standards and guidance

Inter-Agency Network for Education in Emergencies (2010) Minimum Standards for Education: Preparedness, Response and Recovery, second edition. INEE. New York, USA.

Inter-Agency Standing Committee (IASC) (2007) IASC Guidelines on Mental Health and Psychosocial Support in Emergency Settings. IASC. Geneva, Switzerland.

LEGS (2009) Livestock Emergency Guidelines and Standards. Practical Action Publishing. Rugby, UK.

Norwegian Refugee Council / Camp Management Project (2008) The Camp Management Toolkit. Emergency Capacity Building Project. Oslo, Norway.

Overseas Development Institute (2009) *Stakeholder Analysis*. Overseas Development Institute. London, UK.

Slim, H. and Bonwick, A. (2005) *Protection: An ALNAP guide for Humanitarian Agencies.* Overseas Development Institute. London, UK.

SEEP Network (2013) *Minimum Economic Recovery Standards,* Second Edition. The SEEP Network. Washington DC, USA, and Practical Action Publishing, Rugby, UK.

Sphere Project (2011) *Humanitarian Charter and Minimum Standards in Humanitarian Response,* (The Sphere Handbook) The Sphere Project and Practical Action Publishing, Rugby, UK.

Sivakumaran, Suba (2011) *Market Analysis in Emergencies*. The Cash Learning Partnership (CaLP). Oxford, UK.

World Health Organization and King's College London (2011) *The Humanitarian Emergency Settings Perceived Needs Scale (HESPER): Manual with Scale*. WHO. Geneva, Switzerland and London, UK.

Initiatives

ACAPS
www.acaps.org

ALNAP Evaluative Reports Database
http://www.alnap.org/resources/erd.aspx

Communicating with Disaster-Affected Communities (CDAC)
http://www.cdacnetwork.org/

Humanitarian Accountability Partnership
(HAP-International)
www.hapinternational.org

Joint IDP Profiling Service (JIPS)
www.jips.org

Needs Assessment Task Force (NATF) (includes information about the MIRA)
http://www.humanitarianinfo.org/iasc/pageloader.
aspx?page=content-subsidi-common-default&sb=75

Profiling and Assessment Resource Kit (PARK)
www.parkdatabase.org/

ReliefWeb
www.reliefweb.int

Shelter Centre Library
http://sheltercentre.org/library

The Sphere Project
http://www.sphereproject.org/

Glossary

Accountability

is 'how an organization balances the needs of different groups in its decision-making and activities. Most NGOs have processes in place that will meet the accountability requirements of more powerful groups such as project donors or host governments. In *The Good Enough Guide*, however, accountability means making sure that the women, men, and children affected by an emergency are involved in planning, implementing, and judging our response to their emergency too. This helps ensure that a project will have the impact they want to see.' *(Impact Measurement and Accountability in Emergencies: The Good Enough Guide, The ECB Project, 2007)*

Analysis

is 'the process [or skill] of interpreting "raw" data to identify significant facts, trends and anomalies in order to inform decision-making'. *(UNDAC Handbook, 2013 and ACAPS Training Material, 2014)*

Baseline data

'describes a situation that existed before an event... An event might be a drought or an incident of political upheaval, or it may simply be the first time the indicators were ever measured. You can compare your dataset against the baseline data to see how the situation you're studying appears when weighed against the situation as measured before the event. In other words, baseline data can help you to interpret the impact of an event.' *(PARK Database, Glossary, 2014)*

Capacity

is 'a combination of all the strengths and resources available within a community, society or organization that can reduce the level of risk, or the effects of a disaster.' *(UNISDR Terminology on Disaster Risk Reduction, 2009)*

Clusters

are 'groups of humanitarian organizations, both UN and non-UN, in each of the main sectors of humanitarian action, for example, water, health and logistics. They are designated by the Inter-Agency Standing Committee (IASC) and have clear responsibilities for coordination.' *(IASC – Humanitarian Response Info, 2014)*

Disaggregation

means that data 'is separated. For population data, this refers to data at the individual level, so that you can see each person's information, or to data that is divided into different demographic groups, such as sex or age group.' *(Operational Guidance for Coordinated Assessments in Humanitarian Crises, 2012)*

Driver

is 'a factor which causes a particular phenomenon to happen or develop.' In assessments, we often speak of drivers as an underlying factor or a root cause that is instrumental in driving a crisis, or a possible chain of events, forward. These can be identified when analysing assessment findings and should be defined when describing possible future trends or scenarios. *(Oxford Dictionary, 2014, and ACAPS Technical Brief: Scenario Building, 2012)*

Gender-based violence (GBV)

is any act 'that results in, or is likely to result in, physical, sexual or psychological harm or suffering to women, including threats of such acts, coercion or arbitrary deprivation of liberty, whether occurring in public or in private life.' *(UN Declaration on the Elimination of Violence Against Women, 1993)*

Generalist

is a staff member without specialized skills, whereas a specialist has a qualification or experience in a specific area, for example, a health worker. Generalists can play a crucial role in providing analysis, increasing flexibility and reducing costs. Specialists may still be needed, particularly for more in-depth assessments later. *(ACAPS Training Material, 2014)*

P-Codes

is an abbreviated term for 'Place Code'. Using a location's name as an identifier can easily lead to confusion over spelling when translated into different languages or scripts. 'Place Codes (P-codes) are unique alpha-numeric codes that identify locations. All organizations using these codes can easily share data. P-codes are similar to zip codes and postal codes and can form part of a data management system that provides unique reference codes to thousands of place locations. These codes provide a systematic means of linking and exchanging data and analysing relationships between them.' *(PARK Database, 2014, and OCHA – Quick Guide for Cluster Leads, 2007)*

Primary data

'is most generally understood as data gathered from
the information source and which has not undergone
analysis before being included in the needs assessment. Primary data is collected directly from the
affected population by the assessment team through
field work. Primary data is most often collected
through face to face interviews or discussions with
members of the affected community, but can also be
gathered through phone interviews, radio communication, email exchange, and direct observation.' *(ACAPS
Technical Brief: Qualitative and Quantitative Research
Techniques for Humanitarian Needs Assessment: An
Introductory Brief, 2012)*

Purposive sampling

is 'where you choose your sample – i.e., where you will
visit and who you will talk to – with a specific purpose
or with one or more specific predefined groups in
mind.' *(ACAPS Technical Brief: Purposive Sampling
and Site Selection, 2011)*

Qualitative information

is 'virtually any information that is not numerical in
nature and is difficult or even impossible to quantify.
Qualitative data are often *textual* observations that
portray attitudes, perceptions or intentions. They are
typically expressed as words, rather than numbers, and
are used to describe and provide meaning and context
to a situation – the story behind the statistics ... qualitative data have a unique perspective – a view from
inside – and answer questions such as how? And why?

Rather than what? Or how many?' *(WFP, Technical Guidance Sheet #8, Introduction to Qualitative Data and Methods for Collection and Analysis in Food Security Assessments, 2009)*

Quantitative information

'is characterized by the collection of information which can be analysed numerically, the results of which are typically presented using statistics, tables and graphs.' *(ACAPS Technical Brief: Qualitative and Quantitative Research Techniques for Humanitarian Needs Assessment: An Introductory Brief, 2012)*

Secondary data

'is information which has typically been collected by researchers not involved in the current assessment and has undergone at least one layer of analysis before inclusion in the needs assessment. Secondary data can comprise published research, internet materials, media reports, and data which has been cleaned, analysed and collected for a purpose other than the needs assessment, such as academic research or an agency or sector specific monitoring reports.' *(ACAPS Technical Brief: Qualitative and Quantitative Research Techniques for Humanitarian Needs Assessment: An Introductory Brief, 2012)*

Spatial data

is any data that can be mapped, or 'information about locations and shapes of geographical features and the relationships between them, usually stored as coordinates and topology.' *(ESRI GIS Dictionary, 2014)*

Vulnerability

is a set of 'conditions determined by physical, social, economic, environmental and political factors or processes which increase the susceptibility of a community to the impact of shocks/hazards.' *(UNISDR Terminology on Disaster Risk Reduction, 2009)*

For your notes